FOOTBALL SUPERSTARS

MARTENS
RULES

Hi, pleased to meet you.

We hope you enjoy our book about Lieke Martens!

I'm **VARbot** with all the facts and stats!

SIMON   DAN

W

WELBECK

THIS IS A WELBECK CHILDREN'S BOOK
Published in 2022 by Welbeck Children's Books Limited
An imprint of the Welbeck Publishing Group
20 Mortimer Street, London W1T 3JW
Text © 2022 Simon Mugford
Design & Illustration © 2022 Dan Green
ISBN: 978-1-78312-636-1

Writer: Simon Mugford
Designer and Illustrator: Dan Green
Design manager: Sam James
Commissioning editor: Suhel Ahmed
Production: Arlene Alexander

A catalogue record for this book is available from the British Library.

Printed in the UK
10 9 8 7 6 5 4 3 2 1

Statistics and records correct as of April 2022

FOOTBALL SUPERSTARS

MARTENS

RULES

SIMON MUGFORD   DAN GREEN

CONTENTS

MARTENS, MARTENS!

Get ready to meet

LIEKE MARTENS!

The sensational Dutch midfielder is a **EUROS champion** and winner of the **TREBLE** with **Barcelona**.

6

Martens is a footballing phenomenon – and this book is all about her!

Dribbling

One of the best at getting past opponents with the ball at her feet.

Crossing

Lieke's crosses, especially from the left wing, are fast and accurate.

Speed

She outpaces her opposition as she powers down the wing.

Creativity

Tricks and unexpected moves keep her opponents guessing.

Positioning

Creates space and gets into the best positions to receive the ball.

GOALS, GOALS, GOALS!

Lieke is awesome at scoring AND creating opportunities for her team-mates.

MARTENS IN NUMBERS

Lieke has some great numbers to her name . . .

22 . . . her **BARCELONA** shirt number

3 . . . **LEAGUE CHAMPIONSHIPS**

10 . . . **DOMESTIC CUP** wins

149 . . . **CAREER CLUB GOALS**

131 ... **CAPS** and

54 **GOALS** for the **NETHERLANDS**

1 ... **CHAMPIONS LEAGUE** win

1 ... **FIFA BEST** Women's Player Award

1 ... **UEFA** Women's Player of the Year Award

Over **1.3 MILLION**

followers on Instagram!

MARTENS I.D

NAME: *Lieke Elisabeth Petronella Martens*

NICKNAME: *"The Queen"*

DATE OF BIRTH: *16 December 1992*

PLACE OF BIRTH: *Bergen, Netherlands*

HEIGHT: *1.70 m*

POSITION: *Midfielder / winger*

CLUBS: *Heerenveen, VVV-Venlo, Standard Liège, Duisburg, Kopparbergs/Gothenburg FC, Rosengard, Barcelona*

NATIONAL TEAM: *Netherlands*

LEFT OR RIGHT-FOOTED: *Both*

CHAPTER 2

LITTLE LIEKE

Lieke Martens was born in **1992** in **Bergen,** a small town in the eastern **Netherlands,** close to the border with Germany.

NORTH SEA

U.K.

Amsterdam

BERGEN

Ipswich

NETHERLANDS

Düsseldorf

Brussels

BELGIUM

GERMANY

FRANCE

Luxembourg

Paris

Lieke lived in Bergen with her family.

There was her mum, **Thea** . . .

Her dad, **Bert** . . .

And her two older brothers, **Sjoerd** and **Jelle.**

Lieke has a younger sister, *Meike,* too.

Little Lieke spent lots of time **playing games** with her brothers.

There was one game that Lieke and her brothers liked to play more than anything else . . .

FOOTBALL!

BOP!

The three of them would play for **hours** and **hours** in their back garden.

Sjoerd and Jelle would make Lieke go in **goal.** She was never happy about that!

Lieke would carry a ball with her **ALL THE TIME.**

She played football with her brothers and friends in the **park** and in the **street outside her house.**

Everyone in Bergen knew the **little girl footballer** with her long ponytail.

Lieke's house backed on to some fields and the pitch of the local football club, **RKVV Montagnards.**

Lieke and her brothers found a gap in the fence and would **sneak in** and play football on the **training pitch . . .**

Until the caretaker **chased** them away!

"THE BEST THING WAS OF COURSE TO PLAY FOOTBALL . . . WITH MY BROTHERS AND THE BOYS FROM THE NEIGHBOURHOOD. YOU LEARN THE MOST BY PLAYING TOGETHER."

Lieke Martens

CHAPTER 3

HEROES AND DREAMS

25

Every young footballer dreams of playing for
their **favourite team.**
For Lieke, her team
was the Amsterdam
side, **Ajax.**

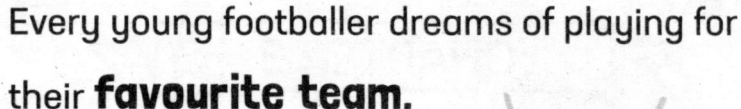

Her bedroom was covered in Ajax posters, and she **ALWAYS** wore her Ajax tracksuit.

Ajax won the Champions League in **1995**, when Lieke was two years old.

27

Lieke supported Ajax when she was little, but her biggest football hero at the time played for **Barcelona** . . .

Lieke pretended to be **Ronaldinho** when she played, copying his awesome dribbling skills and amazing runs down the wing.

ZIP!

Ronaldinho wore his long hair in a ponytail, just like Lieke!

When she was **five,** Lieke was able to join **RKVV Montagnards.** Now she could play there without sneaking through the fence!

Her **brothers** played at the club already and her **dad** helped out with **coaching.**

Lieke could train and play football with her **family and friends. Perfect!**

Lieke was always the **ONLY GIRL** playing. And she was often the **best** player on the pitch.

As Lieke sped down the wing, dribbling the ball past boys **older and bigger** than her, they would shout and even pull her hair.

But that just made Lieke a **faster** and even **better** player.

"TO BE ABLE TO WEAR THE SAME FC BARCELONA COLOURS AS MY HERO STILL MAKES ME SMILE EVERY TIME I THINK ABOUT IT."

Lieke Martens on her childhood idol, Ronaldinho.

RONALDINHO

34

CHAPTER 4

HISTORY LESSONS

Lieke plays in a world of women's football that is slowly growing becoming more and more popular. But it wasn't always that way . . .

Dick, Kerr Ladies was a team from Preston in England, formed in **1917.** They played men's and women's teams – to crowds of more than **50,000** – and toured the USA.

Then the English Football Association

BANNED women's football from its clubs.

In the 1970s, things began to **change.**

The English FA *finally* lifted its ban.

A women's league in **Italy** featured part-time

professional players for the first time.

In **1971,** France and the Netherlands played the first **OFFICIAL** women's international match.

France won **4-0**

The first **OFFICIAL** international tournament – the AFC Women's Championship – was held in Asia in **1975.**

The women's **EUROS** began in **1984.**

Sweden won, but Germany have won it

EIGHT times since.

The Netherlands , with Lieke in the team, won

the EUROS for the first time in **2017.**

There's more about
this later in the book!

The first women's **World Cup** was held in China in **1991.** It was won by the **USA.**

The USA have won the World Cup **four** times - more than any other team.

WOMEN'S LEAGUES TIMELINE

1968 – Italy
Serie A Femminile

1974 – France
Division 1 Féminine

1988 – Spain
Primera Iberdrola

BIRGIT PRINZ,
Frankfurt / Germany

1990 – Germany
Frauen-Bundesliga

ALEX SCOTT,
Arsenal / England

2010 – England
Women's Super League

2012 – USA
National Women's Soccer League

CHAPTER 5

BiG MOVES

In **2005,** when Lieke was **13,** she made the first move of her footballing life. She joined **Olympia '18**, a club in Boxmeer, just a few miles from her home.

Lieke got better and better, outsmarting most of the boys she played against.

She also met **Kika van Es,** Lieke's future Netherlands team-mate and one of her best friends.

While Lieke was an Olympia '18 player, she received a very exciting **invitation** - a trial for the Netherlands **under 15 team!**

Lieke scored in the trial match - **BOOM** - and was selected to play against **Belgium.**

Her friend **Kika** and two other future Netherlands stars, **Stefanie van der Gragt** and **Vanity Lewerissa** were in the squad, too!

Kika, FC Twente defender

Stefanie, Ajax defender

Vanity, Ajax midfielder

2008 was a **BIG** year for Lieke. Aged **15,** she left home to move to **Amsterdam!**

She was going to study – and play lots of **football** – as part of a scheme to develop Dutch girl footballers.

Lieke had to do her own cooking and washing . . . and at first she was **homesick.**

But she soon made lots of friends - and had an **awesome time!**

WHOOP!

At weekends she went home and played for *Olympia '18.*

"I'M SO GLAD I WENT TO AMSTERDAM AT A YOUNG AGE. BECAUSE AS HARD AS IT WAS SOMETIMES, IT HAS MADE ME STRONGER . . ."

Lieke Martens

50

CHAPTER 6

FIRST TEAMS

Lieke was **16** when she finished college in **2009.** It was time to find a professional club!

She joined **Heerenveen** and played her first matches in the **Eredivisie,** the top women's league in the Netherlands.

Lieke played **18 matches** for Heerenveen and scored two goals - one against **Utrecht** and another against **FC Twente**.

Heerenveen finished the season bottom of the league.

In 2010, Lieke joined the newly formed **VVV Venlo.** The club is based just a few miles from her hometown.

And **Kika** joined the club, too!

Lieke's first goal for Venlo was a **penalty** -

against her old club Heerenveen!

Lieke scored **NINE goals** in **20 games** for Venlo.

2011 saw the start of a new season and big step for Lieke. She moved across the border to join the top **Belgian** side **Standard Liège**.

IT WAS HER FIRST PROPER PROFESSIONAL CONTRACT!

Lieke **scored twice** in her first match, a 4-1 win over **FC Twente** to win the **BeNe Super Cup.**

Lieke's *first* professional *trophy!*

Lieke also made her **Champions League** debut, scoring a penalty against Danish side **Brondby.**

LIEKE AT LIÈGE 2011-12

COMPETITION	GAMES	GOALS
FIRST DIVISION	25	17
SUPER CUP	1	2
CHAMPIONS LEAGUE	2	1
TOTAL	28	20

AND LIÈGE WON THE LEAGUE, BRINGING LIEKE HER FIRST CHAMPIONSHIP MEDAL.

LIEKE WAS ON THE UP!

Lieke played matches all over **Europe** for the **Netherlands youth teams . . .**

FOUR GAMES FOR THE UNDER-16s

BOFF!

17 GAMES FOR THE UNDER-17s

The Netherlands had only one shirt size for outfield players at each age group, **LARGE.**

> So Lieke played in a shirt that was way too big!

> HUH!

In **2010,** Lieke, still only 17, was selected for the **under-19s** and played in a major international tournament ...

2010 UNDER-19 EUROPEAN CHAMPIONSHIP

GROUP B

24 MAY 2010

NETHERLANDS 2-0 FRANCE

*Lieke started on the bench against the favourites, but came on after 30 minutes. Within a minute, she headed in a corner – **GOAL!***

WHOMP!

27 MAY 2010

MACEDONIA 0-7 NETHERLANDS

*Lieke started the match in style, **scoring** in the first minute and then slotting home the **sixth goal** as the host nation were thrashed.*

30 MAY 2010

SPAIN 0-2 NETHERLANDS

*Spain were stiffer competition, but Lieke was on the scoresheet again with her **fourth goal** of the competition – **BOOM!***

NEXT UP – THE SEMI-FINALS . . .

It was a very tight game against **England,**

the reigning **champions.** The match went

to **extra-time** and then the dreaded

penalty shoot-out!

Lieke's team missed their second penalty, but she stepped up and confidently **scored the third – *YES!***

FWUP!

But it was not to be. England didn't miss a penalty and were through to the **final.**

Lieke ended as joint top-scorer with **four goals** and named as one of the **TOP TEN** players of the tournament.

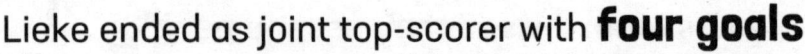

THE 17-YEAR-OLD LIEKE HAD A BRIGHT FUTURE AHEAD.

CHAPTER 8

MARTENS MOVES

In **2012,** Lieke signed for the **German club Duisburg.** They were one of the most successful women's teams in Germany and had recently won the **UEFA Women's Cup.**

And . . . Duisburg is just over the border from Lieke's family in Bergen. **It was perfect!**

But it turned out the club had **problems** with money and contracts. It didn't work out for Lieke at Duisburg and she left after just two seasons.

In 2014 Lieke moved to another club, in another country - **Göteborg** in **Sweden**. The main league there is the **Damallsvenskan**.

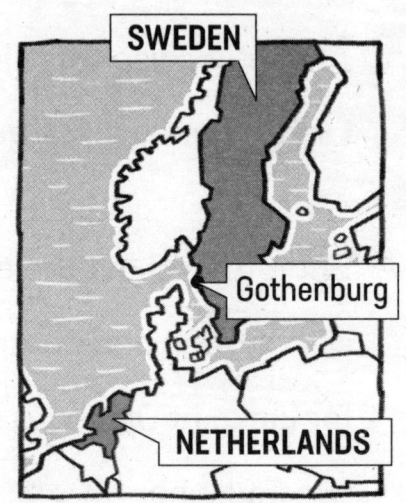

SWEDEN

Gothenburg

NETHERLANDS

She quickly settled in at Göteborg and formed a fearsome attacking partnership with her fellow Dutch team-mate **Manon Melis**.

DUMPF!

Other clubs noticed how well Lieke was playing in the **Damallsvenskan** with Göteborg. In **2015,** she signed for **FC Rosengård.**

AT ROSENGÅRD, LIEKE:

WON THE SWEDISH CUP

Swedish Cup trophy

WON THE SWEDISH SUPERCUP

REACHED THE QUARTER-FINALS OF THE CHAMPIONS LEAGUE

LOST TO BARCELONA

Rosengård have won the Damallsvenskan **12 times** and the Swedish Cup **five times**.

73

LIEKE IN GERMANY AND SWEDEN

DUISBURG	GAMES	GOALS
2011-14	35	11

GÖTEBORG	GAMES	GOALS
2014-15	39	12

ROSENGÅRD	GAMES	GOALS
2016-17	44	25

CHAPTER 9

LEGENDS AND RIVALS

Lieke Martens is one of **THE GREATS** of women's football. Meet some of the others:

ADA HEGERBERG

The Norway striker is a **FIVE-times** Champions League winner with Lyon and the competition's all-time top scorer. Hegerberg won the first women's **Ballon d'Or** in 2018.

MIA HAMM

The USA forward won the first **Women's World Cup** in 1991 and dominated the game for a decade, scoring **158 goals** in 276 games for her country.

MEGAN RAPINOE

The USA's Rapinoe is both a brilliant midfielder and an activist for LGBT rights. She won the **Women's World Cup** in 2015 and 2019, **Olympic gold** in 2012 and the 2019 **Ballon d'Or.**

MARTA

The prolific Brazilian forward has scored more World Cup tournament goals (17) than any player, male or female. She won the The **Best FIFA Women's Player** award in 2018.

SAM KERR

The Australian is one of the most dangerous goalscorers in the modern game, winning the **Golden Boot** in three different leagues.

LILY PARR

As a player in the **Dick, Kerr Ladies** team (see page 36), Parr was known for her powerful shooting. It is believed she scored more than **900** goals in a career that spanned more than 30 years.

LINDA MEDALEN

The tough and versatile Norwegian won **Women's EURO 1993** as a striker and the 1995 **Women's World Cup** as a defender.

CARLI LLOYD

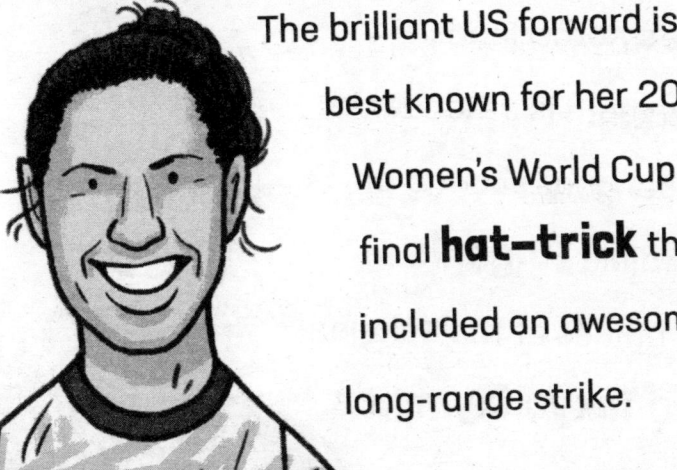

The brilliant US forward is best known for her 2015 Women's World Cup final **hat-trick** that included an awesome long-range strike.

BIRGIT PRINZ

Throughout the 90s and 2000s, the striker was phenomenal, winning **multiple trophies** with Eintracht Frankfurt and Germany.

VIVIANNE MIEDEMA

Lieke's Netherlands team-mate is a wonder in front of goal, scoring an incredible **10 goals** in four games at the delayed 2020 **Tokyo Olympics**.

FRAN KIRBY

The superb England forward is **quick and clever,** and alongside Sam Kerr at Chelsea makes for a dangerous duo.

WENDIE RENARD

The formidable Lyon **defender** is also a
brilliant attacking player, scoring
29 goals for France.

LUCY BRONZE

England's Bronze is a fantastic attacking full-back and winner of the **Champions League** with Lyon and was the **Best FIFA Player in 2020.**

ALEXIA PUTELLAS

The Spanish sensation plays alongside Lieke at **Barcelona** and is the winner of multiple trophies and awards.

CHAPTER 10

BARCELONA

In **2017,** Lieke joined one of the biggest

football clubs in the world . . .

BARCELONA

MARTENS

22

The Spanish side were building a women's team to match the famous men's side and win the **CHAMPIONS LEAGUE.**

MESSI

INIESTA

XAVI

CRUYFF

Lieke and players like **Alexia Putellas** were part of the plan.

In her first **two seasons**

at Barcelona, Lieke . . .

Scored **28 GOALS** . . .

BOOM!

Won the

Spanish Cup . . .

Played against Barca's **BIGGEST** rivals

Atlético Madrid in front of a crowd

of **60,739** . . .

And reached the Champions

League **FINAL!**

Lieke was injured at the start of the **2019–20** season and then . . . football stopped because of the **Coronavirus pandemic.**

Barcelona were named champions when the season was cancelled, so Lieke won her first **Primera División** title . . .

90

CHAPTER 11

ORANGE SENIOR

Lieke made her **senior debut** for the Netherlands in **2011** in a friendly against China.

In 2014, the Netherlands reached the play-offs for the **2015 Women's World Cup**.

Lieke scored in **BOTH legs** against Scotland . . .

AWESOME!

BLAM!

And then they beat **Italy** - Lieke

and the team were off to **Canada**

for their **first ever** World Cup!

WORLD CUP WONDER GOAL

6 JUNE 2015

WOMEN'S WORLD CUP GROUP A

COMMONWEALTH STADIUM, EDMONTON

NETHERLANDS 1-0 NEW ZEALAND

This was the Netherlands, **FIRST** World Cup game. The sun was shining and a crowd of more than **50,000** had turned out to watch.

It was a **BIG** day for Lieke and her team-mates.

In the 33rd minute, Lieke picked up a pass from **Vivianne Miedema,** looked up and **POW** - fired the ball into the back of the net! Her country's first World Cup goal was a

SCORCHER!

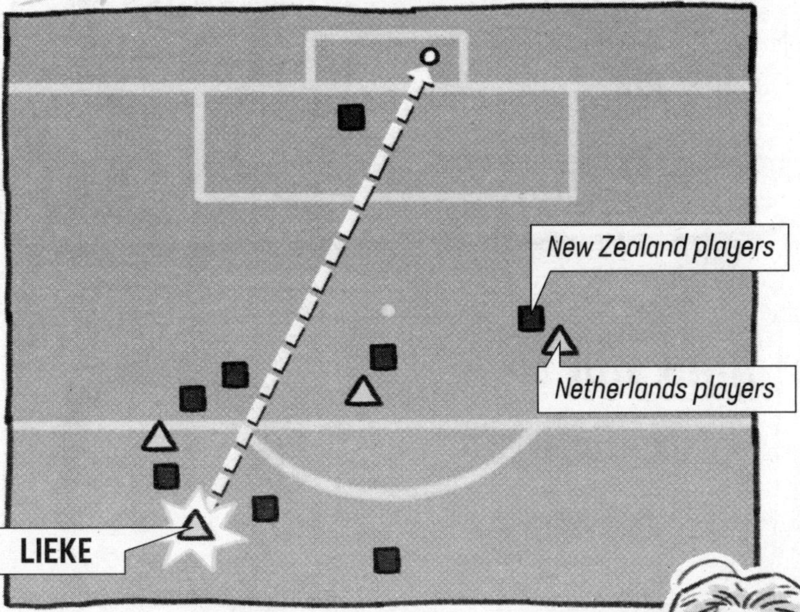

New Zealand players

Netherlands players

LIEKE

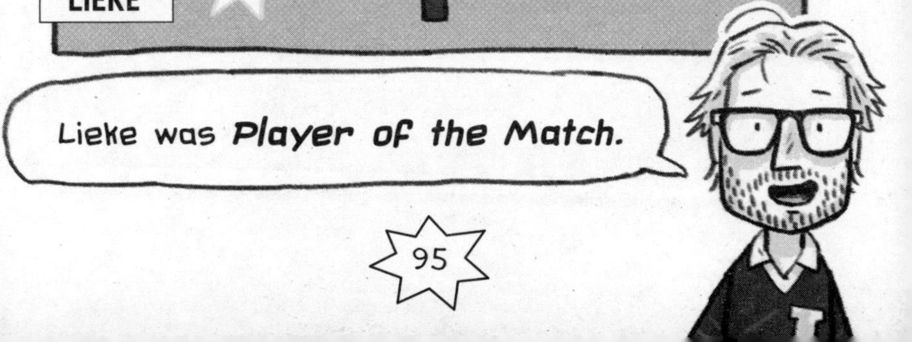

Lieke was *Player of the Match.*

TOP SQUAD

SOME OF LIEKE'S STAR NETHERLANDS TEAM-MATES.

VIVIANNE MIEDEMA

POSITION: **FORWARD**

CLUB: **ARSENAL**

CAPS: **107**

GOALS: **91**

KIKA VAN ES

POSITION: **DEFENDER**

CLUB: **FC TWENTE**

CAPS: **76**

GOALS: **0**

DANIËLLE VAN DE DONK

POSITION: **MIDFIELDER / WINGER**

CLUB: **LYON**

CAPS: **123**

GOALS: **32**

SHERIDA SPITSE

POSITION: **MIDFIELDER**

CLUB: **AJAX**

CAPS: **198**

GOALS: **43**

Why is **Cinderella** rubbish at football?

Because she keeps running away from the **ball!**

GROAN!

TOP SCORERS

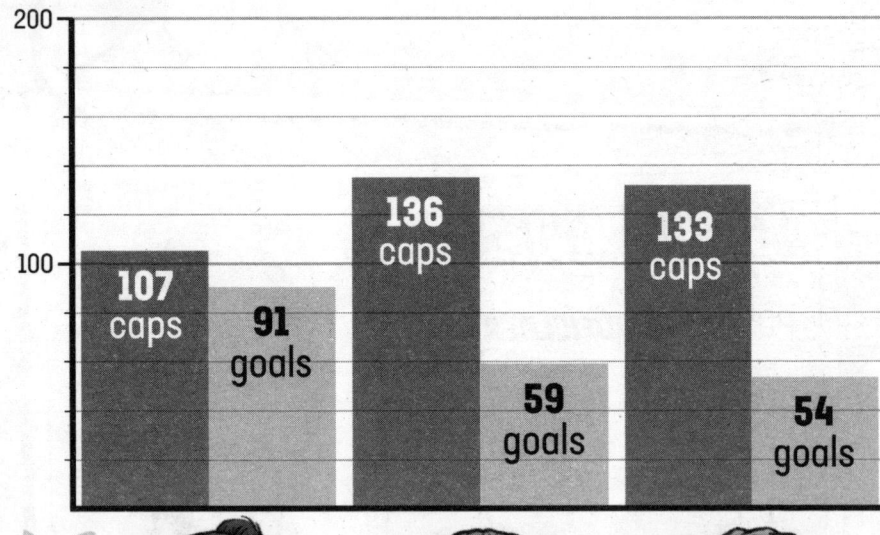

107 caps — Vivianne Miedema
91 goals

136 caps — Manon Melis
59 goals

133 caps — Lieke Martens
54 goals

VIVIANNE MIEDEMA
2013-

MANON MELIS
2005-2016

LIEKE MARTENS
2011-

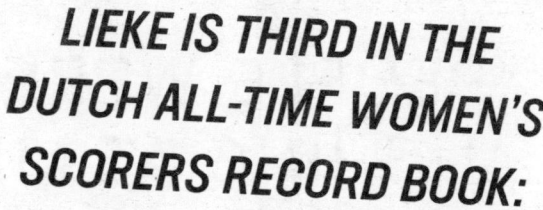

LIEKE IS THIRD IN THE DUTCH ALL-TIME WOMEN'S SCORERS RECORD BOOK:

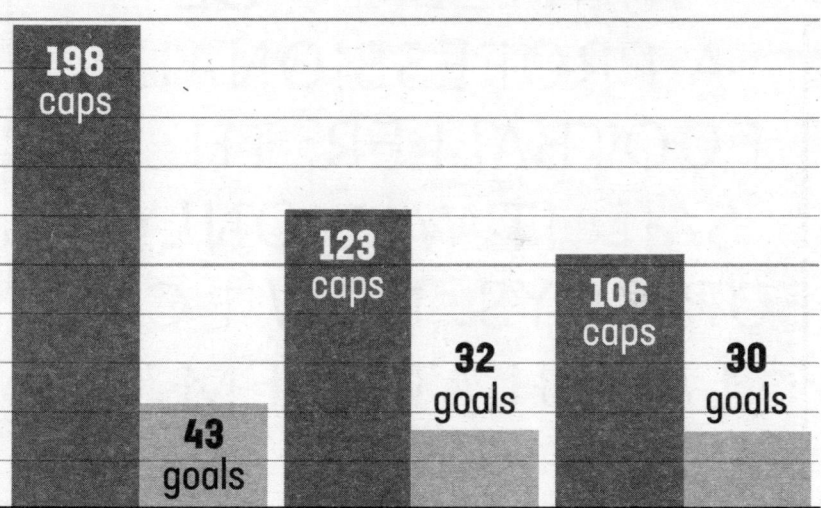

198 caps

123 caps

43 goals

32 goals

106 caps

30 goals

SHERIDA SPITSE
2006-

DANIËLLE VAN DE DONK
2010-

SYLVIA SMIT
2004-2013

"PEOPLE WERE LAUGHING AT ME WHEN I SAID I WANTED TO BE A PROFESSIONAL FOOTBALLER, THEY SAID IT WAS ONLY FOR BOYS. NOW I CAN LAUGH AT THEM."

Lieke Martens

100

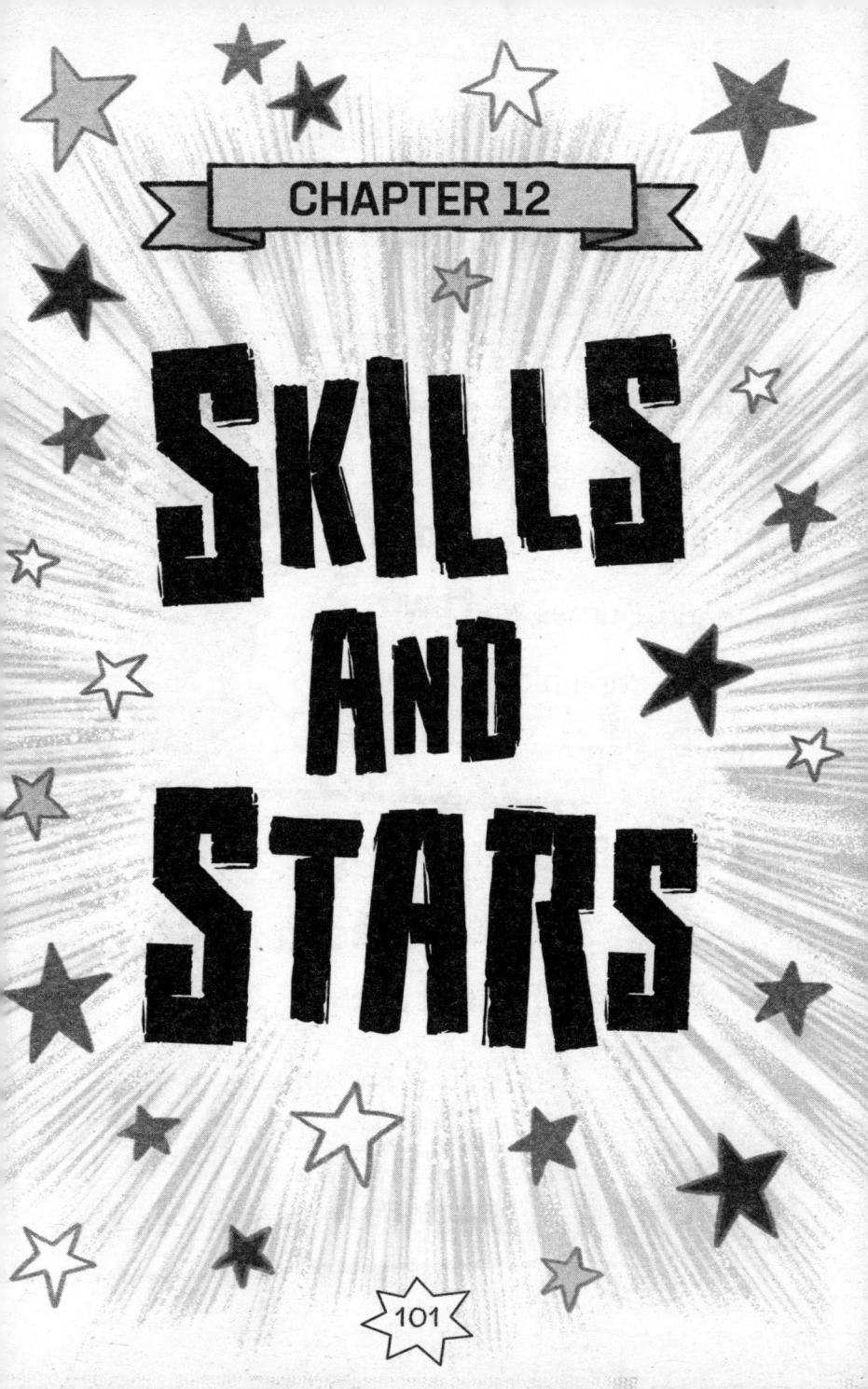

CHAPTER 12

SKILLS AND STARS

Lieke is a brilliant, creative midfield player whose **skills and tricks** are up there with the best in the business.

JOHN BARNES *1981-99*

Born in Jamaica and a **Liverpool** and **England** legend, Barnes won **two** league championships and two FA Cups.

DAVID BECKHAM *1992-2013*

The **Manchester United** and **Real Madrid** midfield master won **six** Premier League titles, two FA Cups, the Champions League and La Liga.

ROBERT PIRES *1993-2015*

Alongside Thierry Henry, Pires helped a great **Arsenal** side win **two** Premier League titles and **two** FA Cups.

CRISTIANO RONALDO *2002-*

The winger turned forward is a **living legend** for fans of **Manchester United, Real Madrid** and **Juventus** – and the Champions League top scorer (141).

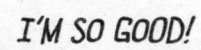

I'M SO GOOD!

THE FEMALE MESSI

When Lieke first wore the famous Barcelona shirt and showed the world her awesome skills - creating space, dribbling and scoring goals - she was immediately compared to **Lionel Messi.**

CRUYFF'S GIRL

Legendary Dutch player **Johan Cruyff** is largely responsible for the style of football played by both the Netherlands and Barcelona today. Lieke even performed the **Cruyff Turn** at the 2019 Women's World Cup.

The Barcelona women's team play at the **Johan Cruyff Stadium**.

"WELL, WE ARE BOTH TECHNICAL AND GOOD AT DRIBBLING. BUT HEY, MESSI COMES FROM ANOTHER PLANET. I DON'T THINK ANYONE CAN COMPARE TO MESSI."

Lieke Martens on being compared to Messi.

CHAPTER 13

THE BEST

107

The **2017 Women's EUROS** were hosted by the Netherlands. The country was buzzing with excitement as Lieke and the team played a major tournament at **HOME**.

16 JULY 2017

GROUP A

NETHERLANDS 1-0 NORWAY

*Lieke's assist for the goal got the hosts off to a **winning start**.*

PLAYER OF THE MATCH

24 JULY 2017

GROUP A

BELGIUM 1-2 NETHERLANDS

*Lieke scored the **winner** as the Netherlands **topped the group**.*

29 JULY 2017

QUARTER-FINAL

NETHERLANDS 2-0 SWEDEN

*It was the **Martens** and **Miedema** show with a goal in each half.*

6 AUGUST 2017

EURO 2017 FINAL

NETHERLANDS 4-2 DENMARK

After beating **England 3-0** in the semis, the Netherlands were in **THE FINAL.**

It didn't start well. Denmark were ahead through a **penalty** within **five minutes. Vivianne Miedema** quickly equalised and then . . .

WHOMP!

Lieke put them ahead with an **AWESOME** left-footed shot –

WOOHOO!

The pulsating match ended **4–2** – the Netherlands were

EUROPEAN CHAMPIONS.

Lieke was amazing at the EUROS:

Three goals, **two** assists and named

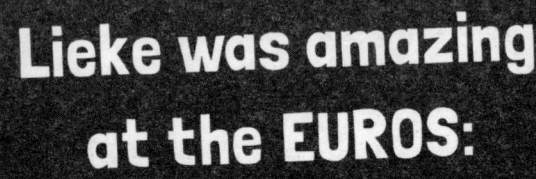

PLAYER OF THE TOURNAMENT

Later that year, Lieke was voted

THE BEST FIFA WOMEN'S PLAYER.

THE BEST PLAYER IN THE WORLD

Cristiano Ronaldo was The Best Men's Player.

OF COURSE!

Lieke played at the **2019 Women's WORLD CUP,** despite having an injured toe. She even scored **TWO GOALS** against Japan!

The Netherlands went all the way to the **FINAL,** but lost 2-0 to the **USA.**

Lieke scored **FOUR** goals at the delayed **2020 OLYMPIC GAMES** before their quarter-final defeat.

The *USA*, again.

BARCELONA 2020-21

ONE INCREDIBLE SEASON

4 OCTOBER 2020

PRIMERA DIVISIÓN

REAL MADRID 0-4 BARCELONA

This was the first women's **EL CLASICO** derby. Lieke scored the third goal as Barça started the season in style.

FWOMP!

11 NOVEMBER 2020

PRIMERA DIVISIÓN

BARCELONA 3-0 ATLÉTICO MADRID

*A **BIG** win over their biggest rivals for the league title and Lieke was on the scoresheet again.*

2 MAY 2021

CHAMPIONS LEAGUE SEMI-FINAL SECOND LEG

PSG 1-2 BARCELONA (3-2 agg)

*Lieke's **two** goals sent Barcelona through to the **Champions League** final against **Chelsea**.*

TREBLE TIME

Barcelona won the league **25 POINTS** clear of Real Madrid.

Lieke's superb dribbling and assists helped them beat **Chelsea 4–0** to win the **Champions League.**

And then . . . Levante were beaten **4–2** to win the **Copa del Reina –**

A HISTORIC TREBLE WIN

to end an incredible season –

LIEKE'S BARCELONA RECORD AND HONOURS

SEASON	GAMES	GOALS
2017-18	38	14
2018-19	31	14
2019-20	19	2
2020-21	36	20
2021-22	22	20

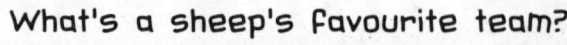

What's a sheep's favourite team?

BAAA-RCELONA!

I DON'T, I SUPPORT
BAAA-RNSTAPLE TOWN!

PRIMERA DIVISIÓN
2019-20
2020-21

CHAMPIONS LEAGUE
2020-21

COPA DE LA REINA
2018
2020
2021

SUPERCOPA FEMENINA
2020

COPA CATALUNYA
2017
2018
2019

QUIZ TIME!

How much do you know about **LIEKE MARTENS?** Try this quiz to find out, then test your friends!

1. Where was Lieke born?

---

2. Which was Lieke's first senior club?

---

3. Which city did Lieke move to when she was 15?

---

4. Which team did Lieke support when she was young?

---

5. Which Brazilian player was her idol?

---

6. With which club did Lieke make her Champions League debut?

----

7. How many cups did she win with Rosengård?

----

8. Against which side did Lieke score her first World Cup goal in 2015?

----

9. How many goals did Lieke score at EURO 2017?

----

10. Which team did Barcelona beat in the 2021 Champions League final?

The answers are on the next page *but no peeking!*

ANSWERS

1. Bergen, Netherlands
2. Heerenveen
3. Amsterdam
4. Ajax
5. Ronaldinho
6. Standard Liège
7. Two
8. New Zealand.
9. Three
10. Chelsea

LIEKE MARTENS:
WORDS YOU SHOULD KNOW

Eredivisie Vrouwen
The top women's league
in the Netherlands.

Frauen-Bundesliga
The top women's
league in Germany.

Damallsvenskan
The top women's
league in Sweden.

Primera División
The top women's
league in Spain.

Copa De La Reina
The main Spanish
cup competition.

HAVE YOU READ ANY OF THESE OTHER BOOKS FROM THE
SUPERSTARS SERIES?

FOOTBALL SUPERSTARS

1 FOOTBALL SUPERSTARS

RONALDO RULES
FACTS · STORIES · STATS
SIMON MUGFORD ★ DAN GREEN

2 FOOTBALL SUPERSTARS

MESSI RULES
FACTS · STORIES · STATS
SIMON MUGFORD ★ DAN GREEN

3 FOOTBALL SUPERSTARS

KANE RULES
FACTS · STORIES · STATS
SIMON MUGFORD ★ DAN GREEN

4 FOOTBALL SUPERSTARS

MBAPPÉ RULES
FACTS · STORIES · STATS
SIMON MUGFORD ★ DAN GREEN

5 FOOTBALL SUPERSTARS

STERLING RULES
FACTS · STORIES · STATS
SIMON MUGFORD ★ DAN GREEN

6 FOOTBALL SUPERSTARS

HAZARD RULES
FACTS · STORIES · STATS
SIMON MUGFORD ★ DAN GREEN

7 FOOTBALL SUPERSTARS

RASHFORD RULES
FACTS · STORIES · STATS
SIMON MUGFORD ★ DAN GREEN

8 FOOTBALL SUPERSTARS

VAN DIJK RULES
FACTS · STORIES · STATS
SIMON MUGFORD ★ DAN GREEN

9 FOOTBALL SUPERSTARS

SALAH RULES
FACTS · STORIES · STATS
SIMON MUGFORD ★ DAN GREEN

10 FOOTBALL SUPERSTARS

NEYMAR RULES
FACTS · STORIES · STATS
SIMON MUGFORD ★ DAN GREEN

11 FOOTBALL SUPERSTARS

AGÜERO RULES
FACTS · STORIES · STATS
SIMON MUGFORD ★ DAN GREEN

12 FOOTBALL SUPERSTARS

POGBA RULES
FACTS · STORIES · STATS
SIMON MUGFORD ★ DAN GREEN

13 FOOTBALL SUPERSTARS

De Bruyne RULES

•FACTS •STORIES •STATS

SIMON MUGFORD ★ DAN GREEN

14 FOOTBALL SUPERSTARS

MANÉ RULES

•FACTS •STORIES •STATS

SIMON MUGFORD ★ DAN GREEN

15 FOOTBALL SUPERSTARS

SouthGate RULES

•FACTS •STORIES •STATS

SIMON MUGFORD ★ DAN GREEN

16 FOOTBALL SUPERSTARS

ZLATAN RULES

•FACTS •STORIES •STATS

SIMON MUGFORD ★ DAN GREEN

17 FOOTBALL SUPERSTARS

HAALAND RULES

•FACTS •STORIES •STATS

SIMON MUGFORD ★ DAN GREEN

18 FOOTBALL SUPERSTARS

MARTENS RULES

•FACTS •STORIES •STATS

SIMON MUGFORD ★ DAN GREEN

19 FOOTBALL SUPERSTARS

BRONZE RULES

•FACTS •STORIES •STATS

SIMON MUGFORD ★ DAN GREEN

COLLECT THEM ALL!

SPORTS SUPERSTARS

1 SPORTS SUPERSTARS

HAMILTON RULES

•FACTS •STORIES •STATS

SIMON MUGFORD ★ DAN GREEN

2 SPORTS SUPERSTARS

RADUCANU RULES

•FACTS •STORIES •STATS

SIMON MUGFORD ★ DAN GREEN

MORE COMING SOON!

ABOUT THE AUTHORS

Simon's first job was at the Science Museum, making paper aeroplanes and blowing bubbles big enough for your dad to stand in. Since then he's written all sorts of books about the stuff he likes, from dinosaurs and rockets, to llamas, loud music and of course, football. Simon has supported Ipswich Town since they won the FA Cup in 1978 (it's true - look it up) and once sat next to Rio Ferdinand on a train. He lives in Kent with his wife and daughter, a dog, cat and two tortoises.

Dan has drawn silly pictures since he could hold a crayon. Then he grew up and started making books about stuff like trucks, space, people's jobs, *Doctor Who* and *Star Wars*. Dan remembers Ipswich Town winning the FA Cup but he didn't watch it because he was too busy making a Viking ship out of brown paper. As a result, he knows more about Vikings than football. Dan lives in Suffolk with his wife, son, daughter and a dog that takes him for very long walks.